"Kathleen Cameron's *Becoming THE ONE* is a transcendent story of empowerment during an unprecedented time. Kathleen's journey of her quantum leap will be sure to inspire and motivate all."

—Peggy McColl,
New York Times best-selling author

"This book skips on the fluff and gets right into the mechanics of co-creating your best life. I couldn't put it down."

—Sabrina Sigalas,
Executive Producer & Creator of COACH the Series

"Kathleen has a powerful, calm presence that is built on absolute belief. She lives what she teaches every day, and she is undeniable proof that it works. *Becoming THE ONE* offers readers a simple but highly effective road map to get from where they are to where they want to be, delivered by an authentic woman who demonstrates by her example that every one of us has the power to choose what our life is and then live it with joy and no apology!"

—Cathy Korpi,
Top Producing Realtor, Springwater, Ontario

"Kathleen Cameron is the 'ultimate coach.' She has been an enormous source of strength and insight for thousands both personally and professionally. *Becoming THE ONE* is a compelling read with an important message.

—Raven Riddle,
Real Estate Mogul and Diamond Academy Advisor

"Experiencing Kathleen's story of waking up to self is one of the most beautiful stories of unfolding. Her honesty and sincerity of the feelings she was going through is easy to understand. This is not a how-to book of strategies to get you aware, but a natural awareness that moves you to better understand our connection to the Infinite! Beautifully written, inspirationally told, and in complete service to the reader for their own journey! A must read!"

—Angie Tumlinson,
Natural Laws Expert

"I highly recommend reading Kathleen's book over and over again! It's a treasure trove of inspiration delivered with love, wisdom and, candour. A true recipe for success."

—Sharon Kempton BMus (Hons), MMus (MusPerf)
Success Coach at Forward Thinking Success Coaching

"Kathleen Cameron is brilliant at weaving together the magic and mystery of manifestation with the realities of her process and her journey. Her authentic, down-to-earth style can help anyone create millions from within."

—Danielle Marggraf,
Master Healer Money, Mindset, and Manifestation Coach, Quantum Healing for Quantum Success

"I couldn't stop reading. Kathleen is telling with her story the whole beauty of the universe: the ease, the magic, and the infinite potential. And the best? Her story is our story. We all are THE ONE. A must read!"

—Kathrin from miss-smarthead.com

"Getting an inside view of the thoughts of an amazing mentor has more value than any strategy on its own. Kathleen has beautifully expressed how she transformed her thinking, which in turn shifted the entire trajectory of her life. Dive deep, study, and implement what Kathleen says in these pages, and you will manifest your dreams."

—Kelly Lephart,
Manifestation & Mindset Coach ~Namaste~

"I love what Kathleen Cameron has done with 'Becoming The One', turning her wounds into wisdom and showing us that anything is possible when you take responsibility, make a decision, and really go for it, the only limitations we have are in our own minds and Kathleen shows what can be achieved when we set goals that stretch us and then get busy achieving them."

—Mark Wilkinson,
International Best selling author - Life Remixed - UK

"Kathleen Cameron's new book *Becoming THE ONE* is an absolute treasure for anyone seeking the secret to abundance, abundance from within. After reading *Becoming THE ONE*, I am left highly motivated, inspired, and truly believing in my own potential. The strength of that belief is fostered by Kathleen herself, who is genuinely leading by example. This is the one book that I will read again and again."

—Dave Falle,
Marketing and IT Manager,
Hasmark Publishing International

"*Becoming THE ONE* by Kathleen Cameron is a remarkable story of one woman's journey to self-enlightenment and finding the power to change her life within herself. It will enable you to tap into your hidden potential and find within yourself everything you need for a successful life."

—Judy O'Beirn,
President & CEO of Hasmark Publishing International

"In this book, Kathleen walks us through her journey and experiences as she discovers her power within. Focusing on keeping her thoughts on 'what she really wants,' she changed her life by improving her self-confidence, using the law of attraction, and the power of faith. She also shows how to use visualization, feelings, and faith, to bring her dreams into the material world. She totally changed her life, becoming THE ONE taking responsibility to change her own circumstances—achieving what she wanted and fulfilling her purpose in life!

—Roberto Delanese,
International Best-selling Author
of *The Delanese Method*

Like Neo in the Matrix, Kathleen wants to know everything…about herself and the Universe. And it paid off. Her outstanding results speak for themselves. Highly inspiring and powerful like her personality. Pick up this book, take a deep breath, and get ready for "Becoming The One!"

—Urusla Perl,
International Best-selling Author
of *Live The U.P. Way*

BECOMING "THE ONE"

KATHLEEN
CAMERON

Hasmark
PUBLISHING
INTERNATIONAL

Hasmark Publishing
www.hasmarkpublishing.com

First Edition

Disclaimer

This book is designed to provide information and motivation to our readers. It is sold with the understanding that the publisher is not engaged to render any type of psychological, legal, or any other kind of professional advice. The content of each article is the sole expression and opinion of its author, and not necessarily that of the publisher. No warranties or guarantees are expressed or implied by the publisher's choice to include any of the content in this volume. Neither the publisher nor the individual author(s) shall be liable for any physical, psychological, emotional, financial, or commercial damages, including, but not limited to, special, incidental, consequential or other damages. Our views and rights are the same: You are responsible for your own choices, actions, and results.

Permission should be addressed in writing to Kathleen at info@diamondacademy.ca

Editor: Brad Green – brad@hasmarkpublishing.com
Cover Design: Anne Karklins – anne@hasmarkpublishing.com
Book Design: Amit Dey – amit@hasmarkpublishing.com

ISBN 13: 978-1-77482-017-9
ISBN 10: 177482017X

Hasmark
PUBLISHING
INTERNATIONAL

Dedication

To my girls, Masyn and Raegan.
Everything I do is for you.

Table of Contents

foreword

The first time I met Kathleen, she came to my studio to receive an award for exceptional performance. Without saying a word, I was struck by the confidence that exuded from her. There was no ego or conceit; it was just pure, beautiful confidence—one that comes from knowing. It was so refreshing. I remember it to this day.

Becoming "The One" is the beautiful and revealing story of dramatic changes that have taken place in Kathleen Cameron's life over the last couple of years. It details how she made a critical paradigm shift that impacted her own life and the lives of her whole family. She records what she learned in this book for others to duplicate. She also coaches individuals to follow the same path.

No stranger to higher learning, Kathleen holds two BAs and a Masters, with a strong background in science. And, as she admits, most who are involved in the realm of science are "show me the proof," and then I'll believe you "kind of individuals." Oddly enough, the changes she made caused her to set aside all questioning and doubt and act on pure faith, which she did and was abundantly rewarded.

This book is a complete guide to changing your life from one of default to one of design. It's an instruction manual to being your best self. It is based on the premise that you have infinite potential, and you are endowed with mental faculties to utilize to turn your dreams into reality.

Regardless of what you have experienced in your life up until now, you can change, and this book will show you how. If you've struggled with confidence, this book is for you. If you've struggled with finances, this book is for you. If you've struggled with making and sticking with your decisions, this book is for you. If you're successful and have dreams that are not yet fulfilled, this book is for you!

By anyone's standard, Kathleen was winning. She's well educated with a loving husband, two beautiful children, a nice home and a great job. But, she wanted more. She was introduced to a coaching program, Thinking Into Results. This program caused an explosion of creativity in Kathleen's mind. What she was learning totally shifted her perception of herself. She began to see herself doing things and having things way beyond what she had experienced in the past and began to understand that she could live all her dreams.

The analytical Kathleen seemed to have been set aside and a new Kathleen full of faith and inspired by huge desires seemed to take over. She began to make quantum leaps in her income. Increases that would normally take a person five to ten years were happening in Kathleen's life in a matter of months.

I have been in the personal development business for going on sixty years. I have seen changes like this in the past, but they are rare. I personally have experienced tremendous change in my life; however, I am totally convinced the changes Kathleen has made and any of the changes I have witnessed in the past have been brought about through faith.

About fifty years ago, I met a man, Clarence Smithison, who shared his definition of faith with me. It's one I have adopted, and I would recommend you adopt as well. It fits Kathleen's situation perfectly. "Faith is the ability to see the invisible, to believe in the incredible. This will cause you to believe what the masses view as impossible."

Kathleen does a beautiful job describing the transitions she made in her mind in going from a life that was happening to her to one she oversaw and actively designed.

It's been written that God will feed every bird, but he will not put food in their nest. Kathleen has a firm grasp of that beautiful truth. Her writing is clear and concise as she questions her innermost beliefs about herself, beliefs that she created and that were created by those who loved her. She explains how she put her ego aside and brought a halt to listening to other people's opinions of her. She delves into how she altered her own self-value and created a new belief about herself that continually serves her and her highest good.

Kathleen Cameron is an extraordinary individual and about as well balanced as anyone I have ever known. I have watched Kathleen make the difficult look easy while creating a beautiful life for herself, her family, and her clients. Kathleen shares the lessons she learned in this book. Now they are yours, but you must apply them to benefit from them.

Bob Proctor

Teacher in *The Secret*
Bestselling Author of *You Were Born Rich*

Introduction

My husband had been asking me to watch the movie *The Matrix* for years. I had zero interest, but one afternoon a few weeks ago I thought *why not?* Many people had told me to check it out, and I was intrigued as to why they were so interested. I watched the majority of the movie feeling like there were many synergies between what I had experienced during the past year of my life and this movie. Although I was not overly engaged in the movie itself, I stayed right up until the final scene, and it was worth the entire watch. Something clicked in me; an understanding and explanation for how I became so powerful so fast.

For anyone who has not seen *The Matrix*, here's a brief explanation. Throughout the film, there is an underlying question of whether or not Keanu Reeves' character, Neo, was "the one." I understood this to mean that Neo was "the one" to change the world—to come in and save the day. You can see throughout the film that there is a constant back and forth where the character Neo is skeptical of himself being labelled "the one," wavering between entertaining the idea and dismissing it altogether. In the final moments of the film, when Neo is fighting for his life, he comes to the realization and finally believes for himself that he is "the one." Along with this realization, he fully grasps the powers that he never knew he had, but that were always there, and he defeats his enemies and saves the day.

This was profound. I, too, have experienced a moment when I came to understand and accept that I was "the one," and that is when all my powers showed up. This potential has always been within me, but like Neo, I was skeptical. In order for it to actually happen, I had to accept it and truly believe it to be true.

CHAPTER 1

A Quantum Leap, or Two...

2020 was a strange year for the world. It was transformative, if you will. It was the same for me, but it was transformative in ways I never would have thought possible. I started the year on a great foot. I had spent three months studying in a course created by Bob Proctor and Sandy Gallagher, two powerhouses in the personal growth and development space. When I started this journey to self-discovery, I hoped for better results in my business, a better home life, and an overall increase in my confidence. I had heard the term "quantum leap" and I thought, I want that quantum leap in my own life. While the decision was not easy, my desire for more was greater than my fear of investing in myself. This was the pivotal moment—the decision which changed my life, and circumstantially for my entire family and my immediate circle.

August 2019 was the month I made the pivotal decision to change my life. I didn't have a bad life. In fact, things were pretty great, but I was not satisfied. I knew I could do more with my life, if only I could see it for myself. I had invested a lot of money in myself before. I had two bachelor's degrees and a master's degree under my belt, so I wasn't afraid of paying to learn. I was doing everything: getting promotions, starting a side business, getting on all the training I could, yet I was making less money than the prior year. I wanted a great life, I wanted to be proud of myself, but things just stayed the same. I came across a training program on "mindset" and immediately was drawn to the topic. I knew almost instantly that whatever it was that this incredible woman was teaching on, I needed to know more about it. I had her on the phone within minutes, and she recommended a course with her and I knew I had to enroll. Then she told me the price and I thought, *well, that's inconvenient.* At first, I thought it was not possible to spend so much, especially since we had just downsized after I resigned from my full-time job. My only income at the time was from my "side hustle." I mentioned it to my husband and he said no, and I thought and thought to myself, *maybe next year*. I sat with this for some time and became sad. I had envisioned a life full of possibility, full of hope, full of confidence and success, and I truly believed it all was possible for me if I was given an accurate road map to follow. I was sad that this was not going to be my story, and I knew I had to revisit it at some point later. I spoke with my husband again, this time not expecting a no, but a yes. I told him why I wanted to better myself, for me, for him, and for our family. He changed his mind and agreed, on one condition—that I would put in the work. I knew I could guarantee that. So, I jumped all in and paid in full with credit. The next six months during the course were nothing short of amazing, and that one decision changed it all.

The next decision at the beginning of January 2020 was the beginning of what would be a giant quantum leap—or several leaps back-to-back—who knows! My side business was growing fast; the work I was doing on myself was paying off. I was accelerating, and my confidence was through the roof. I was so enthralled with everything I was learning, and I would ask myself, "What would I love?" The answer came to me as an intuitive hit, and I didn't listen the first time. But the more I thought about it, the more I knew it was my path. I will never forget the day I had the thought—*what if I could live in this material all day long and help others makes these shifts in their life?*

At a leadership summit in November of 2019, I had the wonderful pleasure of leading a training session on mindset together with a top leader and friend on the team. We both taught for some time, then I led a guided visualization. I played beautiful soft music and led the team of women through the process of visualizing themselves with their goals achieved and then how it felt to have it all, along with the pride in their achievement. When I opened my eyes following the visualization, I felt an instant surge of energy. Every single person there had been impacted by the exercise. The tears, the smiles, and the love in everyone's eyes were palpable. This was one of the first moments I realized that this is truly my purpose.

While the world entered into a global pandemic, I was prepared for my purpose and it all aligned perfectly. It all happened so fast; it seems magical when I look back. I can see now that it was divine timing. Dreams started coming true over and over again. I would ask, and answers would show up. To summarize it most likely won't give credit to the significance of what was happening in my life, but I think it's important to show how much can happen really damn fast when you believe. In 2020, I stepped into my purpose and amplified my life by 2000 times. I improved all aspects of my life—my income, my own business, my home life, friendships, and found the best love of all: self-love. I live a life full of gratitude, joy, spirit, and fun. I am making the impact on others that I always hoped to. The best part is watching my clients' dreams come true right before my eyes! In one year, I built a multi-seven-figure corporation, became a world-leading coach in the mindset space, and built the life for my daughters that I always wanted. This book will expound upon the growth that happened within me so that you can see how it's possible for you to do the same thing. You can create your life by design.

CHAPTER 2

The Reality Is...

How do I put into words the past year of my life? To sum it up in one word would be *extraordinary*.

A little over a year ago, life was happening at a pretty steady rate. I was comfortable with where I was, and I had resigned myself to a normal and acceptable life. I believed life was something that was happening to me; a ride that I was being taken on. I would often ask myself, "I wonder what my future holds?" I remember when my business was not going quite how I hoped it would, and I concluded that it must mean I am not meant for success. I lacked any control over my future, so it's no surprise that nothing was changing for me. I was creating the same day over and over, the same income over and over, and the same level of fulfillment (or lack thereof). The good news is that I never gave up hope of an extraordinary life—and thank goodness I didn't.

This past year I have studied myself more than ever before and I made it my mission to understand the power of my own mind. I have experienced what some would call a paradigm shift—or a quantum leap—but I would rather call it a new perception of reality. The more I studied, the more I started asking questions. Things that had been truths for me for years were starting to unravel. Beliefs that were ingrained in me began to shift, and I started asking, "What if what I have believed all my life isn't true, but rather someone else's version of truth?" I have two science degrees and worked as a nurse for over ten years. For me, truth was evidence-based. Things were only true if you could see its evidence and prove it in a clinical trial. Evidence was the deciding factor, something you could see to prove its validity, reliability, etc. I had gone so far into the "science" of life that spirituality was nowhere to be found. If I could not see something with my own eyes, then it could not possibly be true! This was my reality, the reality I was operating from, so of course, things in life were only as they appeared to be.

Personal growth and development books have been my jam for years, and I have enjoyed a good Tony Robbins event from time to time, but something shifted when I found my mentor and now friend, Bob Proctor. I had read all the books, taken all the free trainings, and yet my life was not showing better results. The conviction behind Bob's message was different. It was strong, and I had to explore it. If what I was doing wasn't working, then maybe pivoting was the answer? I had seen the movie *The Secret* years ago and fell in love with the idea. I remember the story about a gentleman carrying around a gratitude rock in his pocket. Years later, my manager gave me a gratitude rock as a parting gift when I left the company, and it took me right back to that movie. Here I was again, in front of one of the top thinkers in the law of attraction space. This could not just be a coincidence!

I grew up believing that success was possible, but achieving it took hard work and discipline. Both of my parents worked their way up the corporate ladder, and I witnessed things get better for them; a bigger house, a pool in the backyard, a trip to Disneyland, etc. But one day it all ended. My dad, who worked most of his career as CEO and president for one company, was walked off the job. He devoted his life to them, and it was gone in an instant. What I once thought was security didn't seem so secure. This was the first time I thought, *I'd love to work for myself one day*. I had this thought again when my sister got walked off the job a few years later. When I would consider working for myself, thoughts would creep in telling me that it was risky, that I didn't have the knowledge, or that it took a special person to do something like that. I would continue admiring those doing it from afar. One thing I know for sure is that my reality was shifting. Something I once believed was impossible for me was starting to feel possible. As I began learning and growing, my awareness of what was possible became clearer and clearer. My belief in myself and what I wanted to create was being built, one lesson at a time.

The change in my perception of reality was a big one, and it is the reason for the sudden and abundant change in my physical reality. I went from someone who saw herself as being created, to actually being a creator. There is so much power behind the words "choice," "decision," and "creation." These words were not often found in my vocabulary. I now believe that every thought, every emotion, and every action is a choice. I make decisions as an artist painting her canvas, and I now know that I am a creator. My thoughts of today create my tomorrow, and I have taken control of the wheel.

Creation is a powerful part of my life now, and I understand that I am in constant creation with the use of my thinking. I now understand that my thinking is what creates my physical world. The thinking of today creates tomorrow. So, my physical world right now, in this moment, is the product of past thinking. When you really grasp this concept, it becomes life changing. The control you have in your future starts right now with the control of your mind.

The first time I truly felt the weight of this reality was when I attended a training session in February of 2020 as a brand-new coach and consultant. I was programming myself to believe that I was a top coach, that I was top of the leaderboards, and that I had hundreds of clients, but my physical world was lagging behind. I remember seeing all the top coaches being seated at their VIP tables in the front of the room, thinking that I should really be there. They had overlooked me! I remember feeling so uncomfortable because I knew what was on its way—all the success that was manifesting. I couldn't understand why I couldn't just be sitting there among the VIPs! I understand now that all I needed was some patience, but what this shows you is the conviction in my thinking. I KNEW without the shadow of a doubt what the future held for me. How often can one actually say this?

The next time this happened to me was when I manifested my new home. I was living in my imagination all day long in a bright, spacious home, making coffee in my white open kitchen, and then all of a sudden, I would notice that I was actually in my current home, the much smaller, less open, and less modern one. I say now that I was "brought back down to earth." This was just me becoming aware again of my physical world that I was ahead of in my thinking. Your reality is what you decide it to be in your mind. The reality is…you can create anything you want.

CHAPTER 3

Falling in Love with Myself

The funny thing about self-love is that I'm pretty sure we all had it before someone told us otherwise. I truly do believe that it is our natural state. Over the years, we learn to compete and compare, and we become very aware of how we do not match up with others. Growing up as an overweight girl, this message was one I received on repeat. Friends, family, strangers, and the media all told me that my body was "too big" and that I needed to go on a "diet." When I was eleven years old, I would throw out my lunch and starve myself, drinking large amounts of water because someone told me it would "flush the fat out." This narrative continued for almost thirty years. My life has been consumed with aspiring to be the ideal weight—a constant up and down between pride and failure, deprivation and over-indulgence.

In 2018, I made the decision that I was no longer going to be the big girl. I made a decision to lose the weight and get "healthy." Well, I ended up losing 100 pounds and believed that I was finally worthy, finally accepted, and would finally be proud of myself. I felt amazing and my confidence was booming. This feeling of acceptance was joyful, so much so that it hid the hunger, the pressure to be moving all the time, the exhaustion. I had a huge wake-up call when I started dropping to the floor 4-5 times per week. I had made such a drastic change to my body that it couldn't keep up. My heart was telling me that enough was enough. I was told to increase my food consumption and to stop exercising. You can imagine what happened next. The weight started coming back, and so did the feelings of worthlessness, sadness, and fear that those who judged me for so long would be back judging me again.

Looking back, I can see that I left my self-esteem up to others. I only chose to love myself when others loved me. Acceptance was the motive; self-love was the hope. I wanted to be liked by others, but never once thought about liking myself. When I started to change my thinking and began studying the power of the mind, I spent a solid thirty days studying and designing myself. I don't think I have ever spent this much time focused solely on myself. There were highs and lows. I became very aware of how nasty I was to myself, and it took me to a low place. I recognize now that going to this low place was what brought order and clarity for me to resolve the issues that were so deeply ingrained. Having placed so much value on other people's opinions of me, you can only imagine the sudden shift when I put all that focus, all that value onto myself. This was life changing.

A huge shift happened when I heard the idea that we are not our bodies, but that we are *in* our bodies. This was a brand-new thought for me. I had lived my entire life identifying myself by my body. How my body looked consumed so much of my thoughts, and I certainly believed that I was my body and that my body was not beautiful—that it was displeasing to the eye. I walked around for years feeling ashamed and embarrassed. When I chose to accept this new belief, that I am not my body, I suddenly disconnected from the judgement, the hate, the power that my physical appearance had over me and my reactions to my physical world. I stopped letting my body be the reason why I was not successful. The old narrative, "I can't be like her because I'm too fat. I will never be successful like her because she is thin and beautiful," was no longer relevant. Success does not come from my body, but from me, and I hold all the power.

I'm not sure if you will have noticed the real shift that happened here. I started taking responsibility. The love I have for myself is up to me, and I had been giving that control over to others. Whether or not I believed my body was good or bad came from me, not from others. I now know that I am in control of myself and it is a choice to let fabricated beauty standards in from the outside. You can choose to believe that you will never measure up unless you change your appearance, or you can decide that you are a beautiful, powerful being the way you are right now in this moment. I made my choice, and it has been the most liberating decision I have ever made.

Once I let go of this "worthy" ideal set by others and began embracing who I was in that moment in the body I was in, true alignment began to take place. I no longer believed that I needed to change my body in any way; no more waiting for the time "when I lose the weight." I began behaving like the perfect, beautiful, powerful being that I am. My life started to change. People started wanting to work with me, learn from me, and join me on my journey. People were being inspired not because I released weight, but because I accepted myself for who I am, being confident in my plus-size body, showing others how they could live NOW. Some of the best messages I have received came after I released the negativity about my body. One of the most beautiful compliments I ever got was when I was told by someone that I helped them realize they'd used their curvy body as an excuse for why they couldn't excel in their coaching business, and that I had completely proved her wrong. You can be plus-size and successful. You can be curvy and rich. You can be above average size AND love yourself.

What has been very clear is that I had been so used to seeing my negatives instead of my positives. Shifting this perspective was essential. One thing I changed drastically was my inner dialogue. You might not be aware of it, but it's going through your head all day long. Mine sounded like this: "You are not as good as her, so why even bother? You need to lose weight… look how disgusting you look. They can do it because they have what it takes. Life is hard being me." When I started paying attention to my thoughts, I couldn't believe what I heard. I would never say these nasty things to someone else, but I so easily said them to myself. It was appalling, to say the least. If I was putting myself down like this all day long, then why would I ever think I was good enough, or worthy of success?

Your inner dialogue needs to be one that empowers you, raises your vibration, and brings your best quality to light. YOU need to be your own cheerleader. After taking note of my current thoughts, I made the decision to change them. I know this may seem impossible—they come so fast and naturally—but trust me, you have the power. I started telling myself what I needed to hear to change my belief in myself. I started saying things like, "You are beautiful how you are right now," "You are worthy and capable of success," "You are powerful," and "You are inspiring to others." It did not take long before I started to believe it. I made a choice to encourage myself like I would encourage my best friend, my sister, or my mom.

What change can you make today? What is one thing you can tell yourself to encourage yourself to keep going, to take the leap, to dare to be different? This isn't just about loving myself, but being my absolute best version, well past who I am in this physical moment. It's about showing up as the person I want to become.

When I started to achieve success quickly, a friend said something very powerful to me in the perfect moment. She said that this is my new standard, and that I should accept nothing else. This resonated with me deeply. I needed to accept this belief about myself, that I AM capable of great things, and that I have been capable all along. This is not just a fleeting moment, just a lucky couple of months, but it is my true nature, one that I was finally stepping into! We have so much potential within us, but we place limitations on ourselves. I always think of it like a lid on a jar; we won't go further than what we see for ourselves, and yet we never dream as not to get our hopes up. Well, my hopes are up and I'm going for it. I believe most of us have no clue what we are really capable of. This year has proven this to me. Now I know with absolute certainty that the sky is not the limit—we have the entire universe at our disposal.

CHAPTER 4

Being "Undetermined"

The moment I realized I wasn't "determined," it all changed. I'm not sure about you, but most of my life I wished I was different. It was one thing to dislike my body, but disliking my personality was another thing altogether since personality is not something I could change. Or so I thought.

I grew up always believing that I was sensitive. I would get my feelings hurt easily and would end up in tears. This sensitive side of me was something I wished would vanish, but it always stayed. After spending time on myself and digging deep into the person I perceived myself to be, things started to unravel. I began to question things. For years, I believed being sensitive was a bad thing. I vividly remember the day this past year where I thought to myself, *could being sensitive be a good thing?* I had two choices: start affirming to myself that I was the opposite of sensitive, or simply embrace the fact that I am. I started really thinking about this (something I very rarely did before this past year), and I realized that being sensitive has been an asset for me. I am able to connect to the "feeling" of something, a skill I now know is vital in the realization of goals. *Feeling* is what takes an idea and puts it into our programming faster. For example, sadness around failure programs us to believe that we will fail.

Feeling really is the secret to manifesting, and I was good at that! Just like that, I had just changed a belief about myself. I'm not *less than* because I am sensitive—I am *powerful* because I am sensitive. The problem wasn't that I was feeling; it was that I was allowing myself to feel the wrong things. I was affirming the wrong beliefs, ones that were limiting me instead of helping me grow and expand!

When I started in university, I went into every situation with the same level of effort that I did in high school. I believed that I was an average student and expected the same thing to happen in college. It was a shock when I was placed on academic probation and a letter was sent home to my parents letting them know. I had two choices: either accept this fate as my truth, or change it. I chose to change the outcome, and this involved seeing myself differently. I no longer wanted to accept this identity, the identity of being a failure. I made a decision to change, and just like that, I started pulling in straight A's. Since then, I have been what I call a high achiever. A change to my identity had taken place. I continued through life doing well academically, but it would not translate into success in other areas until I made the decision in 2019 to change my entire identity and for good.

This began one of the most transformative times of my life. I did not change, I'm the same Kathleen, but I changed how I see myself. What if I stopped seeing the worst in me and saw the best in me instead? The things I believed were true and didn't like, I simply replaced with how I would want to be. The things I wanted to be, I decided I *was.* I knew that believing I was confident would help me achieve more, so I affirmed confidence. I knew that seeing myself as disciplined would accelerate myself, so I affirmed discipline. I often ask myself, "When I am my highest self, how do I see myself? How do I show up?" This is the real me.

I had heard of the concept of "limiting beliefs" over my years of reading personal development books, and I believed it to be true. I could identify the beliefs that were placing limits on my life, but could not figure out how to change them. The choosing and replacing of these beliefs made all the difference. Magical things started happening when I changed my beliefs about myself. When I started seeing myself as being good at sales, the sales came. When I saw myself as a good leader, people started following my lead. When I started to believe that my mind was powerful, I started changing my physical results around me. Who knew?

Many ask how I changed my beliefs about myself so quickly. I did this through suggestion. The power of suggestion cannot be ignored. There were things I knew I did not believe to be true, but had a feeling that if I believed them, I would be unstoppable. I started suggesting the new belief to my subconscious mind with feeling. I would stand in the mirror and recite affirmations I had written purposefully. I would record my new identity on a voice recorder and listen to it over and over throughout the day. I would take pen to paper and write her out in the present tense. The more I focused on the things I loved about myself, the more things I found to love!

I went from being "determined" to "designed," and nothing will ever be the same. Loving myself right now, in this moment, while always seeking to see myself in the best possible way is the key to continuing to grow myself and my legacy. I would encourage you to do the same. I still have room to grow in this area. I have no doubt about that—but by releasing the idea that I was "born this way," it all changed. I was born a very different way, and once I started to believe in the true greatness within me, everything was different.

I want to share a bit about the powers I believe I have harnessed which have helped me accelerate my life and create my beautiful quantum leap.

CHAPTER 5

Thoughts as Energy

What is a thought? And why can no one hear it but us? We don't often question what thoughts are, since they have been running a mile a minute for as long as we can remember. I only recently started paying attention to thoughts and taking an inventory of the types of thoughts I was having. I would say most of my thoughts were highly unproductive (similar to my behaviour if I'm being honest). When I started paying attention, I also realized that I could control my thoughts. I could let the nagging thoughts of why I didn't like myself run amok, or I could focus on thinking about my future. Huge shocker here—you have control of your thoughts and can choose what you think about. I know, I was shocked too.

After the birth of my second daughter was when my thinking was at its worst. I had a baby at home and a toddler. Nothing bad happened. My life was good, but I was very sad. The more thoughts of sadness I had, the more sad thoughts would continue to come until I was so overcome with sadness that a positive thought had no chance of getting in. I remember telling my husband, "I'm so sad, I can't stop crying and I don't know why." It became a place of despair, so sad that there was no way out but to end it all, I thought. I was so deep in the negative, but I had one thought that changed it all. What if I could get out from under this cloud? What if someone could help me? I remember the day I walked myself and my two kids to the walk-in clinic and told the doctor I was planning how to end my life. He tried to tell me he couldn't help me and that I needed to see my family doctor (which I did not have). I was a nurse, so I knew he could help. I mustered up the last bit of strength I had within me to tell him I needed him to prescribe me something. He did, and within two weeks the cloud was lifted. I was on these medications until last year; my happiness had been dependent on them. As I would try to wean myself off, the sadness returned, just as I expected.

There is good news here. Since studying the mind and the power of our thinking, I trained myself to see the good, to think only of the positive, and to see all my strengths, and by doing so, I was able to stop taking the medication. Thoughts are powerful, and you control them. I learned how to control mine and do the opposite; I fill my mind with nothing but positive thoughts, so the negative has no room to get in. I love the analogy of a garden. I see my mind as the garden: positive thoughts are planted, pruned and watered, and the garden is maintained by pulling the weeds (the negative thoughts) before they can take over.

I went even further in understanding my thoughts and began to consider that thoughts are energy. Thinking this way about my own thoughts really gave me a better sense of responsibility and allowed me to control them more. I remember when I was in psychology class in university, the professor was talking about the phenomenon of thinking about a friend, and then your phone rings and it's that same friend on the line. Or, staring at someone from behind in class and they sense it and turn around. This is thought energy! If every thought sends out energy, if it makes its own impact, then it's vital that we are thinking the right things!

When I visualize—when I think of my higher self, when I connect to source—my thought energy is in alignment with what I want, and never in line with what I don't want. If I am thinking about love, joy, gratitude, and prosperity, that is the energy I am sending out; thus, it is the energy I will receive back.

One of my favourites quotes goes like this: "Do not try to correct in the earth what needs to be corrected in the heavens." I understand this to mean that your results in your life can't be corrected anywhere else but in their origin—your thinking. We can't ask for things around us to be better—we must be better. I have received this message loud and clear.

CHAPTER 6

A Whole New World

The last time I used my imagination was probably around the time I was nine years old. I hadn't given it much thought until I started studying the mind. I couldn't even tell you what the purpose of our imagination was. I never thought I was a creative person, as I used to believe people were either born with creativity or not. What I have come to realize is that we are all born with a creative mechanism and I was simply not using the powerful tool that I was given. A whole new world was opened when I began to really understand and use my imagination.

I first started learning about my imagination when I was guided through a visualization. I was taken on a beautiful journey, seeing myself with all my goals and desires achieved and feeling grateful and proud for all I had accomplished. I was so emotional, tears streamed down my face. How could just thinking of something so wonderful create such a change in me emotionally, and on a molecular level, leading to physical tears? I was intrigued. It felt like I was daydreaming, something we were told to stop doing once we got out of elementary school. I have to admit, it felt really good—but I needed to understand it more. What I was hearing was that by going to the place with my goals achieved using my imagination, I would bring that life into the now. I needed to understand this more, so I took a deeper dive. The scientist in me needed to know.

Here is what I found. Every single thing in our physical world right now was once a thought in someone's mind. These thoughts combine to form a picture. If this picture is held consistently, it will inevitably manifest into the physical form. So, if I create a picture of my dream life and hold it with emotion, then it should manifest in the physical. I thought it was worth a try, so try I did. I started with small things and then practiced with bigger things.

The first thing I tried was coffee. I decided I wanted to bring a coffee into my physical world. I thought about a nice coffee from a local shop and how warm it was in my hands and how comforting it would be to drink. Well, interestingly enough, my cleaning lady came that day and she decided, for the first time ever, to bring me a coffee. Could this have been a coincidence? I was not fully convinced, so I tried this again with a team prize I was hoping to win. I created the picture in my mind of what it would feel like to win this prize. I celebrated in my imagination and it felt so real. I swore it was going to happen. I was going to win! Well, wouldn't you know it? I won! The signs were building and so was my belief. Things that I was picturing in my mind started to show up in my physical world. This was not just a coincidence; I had power. This was now truth to me, and the evidence was strong.

I have now started living in my imagination. I live from the end (the goal) constantly, and even make decisions from there. I see myself as my highest self, the way I am with all my goals achieved, making the impact I have always wanted to make. By using my imagination to go there, I feel the feeling of the wish being fulfilled, I see how I think and behave there, and I raise the frequency I am operating at. And as I leave my imagination, I bring all this to the physical.

I believe my imagination is the gateway to creation. I first decide what I want my life to look like. Then I use my imagination to "live there" in what I call the fourth dimension (often referred to as the quantum realm or the vortex). This type of living creates a forward jump in my physical world towards the fourth dimensional world I have created. It's the merging of the two worlds into one that brings it into this physical world. When I hear myself say these things, it seems almost crazy—a woman with two science degrees talking about multi-dimensions—but it's what I believe, and it works every single time.

I started working on larger things in my imagination (and by larger, I only mean a bit harder to believe). I did this with money, closing sales, my team's production, new business ventures, and more.

One of my favourite manifestations was when I wanted to grow my team. I created an affirmation that I am so happy and grateful now that one new team member joins my team per day. I was used to about 4-6 joining per month, so this was a stretch. I focused on the end result, how it felt when I realized I was having one person join per day. I also started planning for the success—how would I train all the new people coming in and keep them feeling supported? Well, wouldn't you know it, focusing my thought energy on the goal, after about a week and a half of writing it out and visualizing it, it started to happen. I held it for about eleven days with eleven new team members and then I got distracted, went on a trip I earned, and released the focus. This showed me what was possible. I used this exact same strategy to manifest one new coaching client into my business per day. What used to be a $300 sale into my business was now bringing in $7000 per sale—all because I held the belief. The thinking really is the same no matter the value we place on things.

I also remember focusing on my team's performance and noticing they were not being as productive as I would have liked. This was my first mistake. I was asking for more of the same, and I continued to say, "My team is not duplicating." So I started to be really intentional. How do I want this to be? What would I love? I immediately shifted my focus from a team not seeing their success to a team that was booming and growing and so proud of themselves! I began picturing them celebrating themselves, the joy in their faces, seeing them walk across the stage. Not even three months later, I got to stand at the base of the stage and watch multiple members of my team be recognized, just as I had pictured in my mind.

After making such simple manifestations, I asked myself the question, *how do I now bring really big things into my life?* Bob Proctor told me "the process is exactly the same." Once I decide the next manifestation is "really big," I am applying a value to it, which makes it seem harder to do, when in fact it is not. So, I replicated the process, this time for the beautiful car I wanted, then a multi-million-dollar home, and $3,000,000 a year in my first year in business, each million being done in a faster time. He was right—it worked. Now I know the formula and know I can create anything I want.

You don't have to believe me. But what if you did, and what if it worked? Wouldn't that be lovely? Wouldn't that be worth it?

CHAPTER 7

Purity of Mind

While reading one day, I came across the phrase "purity of mind" and it hit me like a ton of bricks. I loved the analogy because it made me think of something that is pure, something that is in the best possible state. Pure gold, a pure diamond, or pure water. It is free from anything negative, anything harsh, and free from contaminants. I loved this idea so much. How can I make sure my mind is as pure as possible? I can do this by making sure I don't let anything in that is not helping me to remain in a state of pure mind.

The first step for me in making sure my mind was always pure was to figure out what I deemed to be unwanted. What are the things that are not serving me, that are lacking in purity? I knew a few things right away: negative self-talk, reacting to other people's opinions, doubting myself, indecision, thoughts of lack, worry, what ifs, etc.

There is so much going on in our mind that has been programmed to be there. We have heard the messages over and over again, so we think about them more and more and eventually, we don't even notice that we are worried, scared, or stressed. We think these are states of being that we have no control over. I know I have been there, in this loop. When I started referring to this as fear-based programming, worry-based programming, indecision-based programming, it reminded me that I can change the program. I can change the pattern.

A pure mind goes even further than what's just in it, but how I choose to see things. The law of relativity is something I make sure I am using to my benefit on a regular basis. We place value on things based on their comparison to other things. A glass looks large when compared with a smaller glass. A road trip seems long when compared to a daily short drive. We can use this law against ourselves all day long if we'd like, comparing ourselves to someone doing it better, someone doing it faster, or someone who looks like they are doing it with greater ease. When we use this to our advantage, we make ourselves feel stronger and more powerful, and we make things appear better. It's all in our perception of something. I have chosen to find the good in most situations and really try to make sure I am the observer of my own thoughts. I know when my vibration is low, and it usually stems from a single thought that is festering. Self-awareness is key.

One of the most important things I have done is to manage my doubts. When you doubt yourself, you are not asking for that thing—you are in a state of resisting it. When you doubt yourself, you attract more things in life to doubt. When you doubt yourself, you are lowering your vibration and impacting what you attract. When you doubt yourself, you are asking for the same over and over again.

I often ask myself, "Could my mind be cleansed a little more? How pure is my thinking right now? Am I in control of my thoughts at this moment?" If I'm not choosing these thoughts, then who is?

CHAPTER 8

Dual forces

There is a misconception that success comes quickly to people when they work really hard for it, or they got lucky. I've had these comments directed at me. "You must be exhausted? I don't want to work as hard as you do." Or, "How did you get so lucky?" I used to believe these things were true also, that success came from either "hard work" or from simply being in the right place at the right time. What I didn't know—and most people don't—is that there is a method behind sudden and exponential growth, and it's not luck or hard work alone. This method or practice is the effective use of two forces used in conjunction with one another that allows for extraordinary results in record time. Essentially, I accelerated myself.

I have always been someone with drive and motivation, somewhat of a high achiever. Once I really started to apply myself in university, I started to realize I could really make it happen. I started to feel smart and that I could likely find myself a good career. I had placed a ceiling on my beliefs, however, and over the years it became evident. I wanted more, but I never really believed I could achieve more. So, I sat in the same place for years. I was always working on several things at one time. I had my first daughter and began a master's degree while on maternity leave. After having my second daughter and finishing my master's, I started a side business. I was in action, but not seeing the results I wanted. Things changed very quickly when I started applying what I refer to as the "dual forces." This duality is the combination of spirituality and peak performance.

The first force (not to be confused with forcing, but rather power) was the movement of my body towards my goal. While I was someone always in activity, I learned quickly that I was in strictly mechanical action. I had not entered into the spirit of the tasks I was doing. I was simply going through the motions of doing the work, but not reaping the full benefits I would have enjoyed had I been present, engaged, inspired, and confident in my outcome. When I started doing these actions from a spiritual place, the results were doubling, then tripling. I started to get more sales, more team members joining me, and more money coming into my bank account consistently.

I also realized another thing: I was not working efficiently. I would spend almost all day working, constantly on my phone, doing this while doing something else at the same time. I was very good at multi-tasking. When I really started to look at how I was spending my time, what I was spending time on, and how engaged I was on each task, I realized there was a more focused and intentional way I could be spending my time. I started working in blocks of four hours per day, and started seeing more results from that four hours. Before long, I was seeing the results of an eight-hour workday from my block of only four hours! I removed non-productive activities, I made sure everything I did was high impact, and I stopped procrastinating. Focused attention is the key here. Spending one hour working on one thing, and one thing alone, was worth hours of time I would have spent prior. I began to realize tasks that used to take me four hours were being done in twenty minutes. I was able to spend more time with my daughters, more time with me, and more time just "being."

The second force I refer to is the magnetic power of bringing my goals closer to me (into the physical). One of my favourite laws of the universe is the law of vibration. I understood this law from science class but now see it from a very different standpoint. Yes, we are all made up of energy and we are all in motion at all times, vibrating and oscillating. What I did not apply into my life, likely because I was not taught to do so, was how this oscillation could help me in attracting what I want in life.

I had a breakthrough when I realized that I am in complete control of the state of vibration I am in. That was a wow moment for me. I know my vibe is not dependent on others, but on me alone.

This is why it is so important for you to train yourself to be happy and to program happiness as your dominant feeling, which we will discuss more in detail later.

My understanding now is quite simple. I control my vibration through my thoughts, feelings, and emotions. How I think, believe, and feel are all ways of either lowering my vibration or raising it. If I am in a sad vibration, or bad mood, I am vibrating at a lower rate, which is caused by my thoughts and beliefs. If I am "vibing high," it's because I am thinking of good things, things I love, and likely how I want things to be. I notice my lower emotions are usually caused when I am thinking about the things I don't want in life, and when I'm feeling good, I am thinking about what I do want in life. But how does this state of vibration attract things into our lives?

I started to question the relevance of my state with bringing things into my life. I had heard about being a vibrational match to all that you desire and thought this was intriguing. Since our feelings or emotions impact the state of our vibration (high or low) and our future desired state has a feeling, it makes sense that we would need to be that feeling now to bring forth the future feeling of the desired state. The term "act as if" has never resonated with me as it feels like pretending, but I see it as being that person, in that vibration NOW. If you feel that it is on its way, if you believe it, you are closer to becoming a match. If you stay on this vibration, if you remain a vibrational match, you will become it, by law. Many of us never believe so we stop thinking of it, and start thinking about what we don't want. Then we are right back at a lower vibrational state, and no longer a match to what we desire.

The icing on the cake, and where true power is put into place, is that your attraction is based on this vibrational state. So, if you are happy, you attract more things to be happy about. If you are grateful, you attract more things to be grateful for. However, if you are critical of others, you are likely critical of yourself and attracting others to criticize you. If you are judging others, you are likely more impacted by other people's judgements of you. If you want to live a life of love and confidence, think of nothing but love and confidence. When you think self-doubt, you are not in alignment with this. You are not a match. The more you give, the more you receive. I have learned this huge lesson, and there is a whole section on it coming up!

Become an observer of your thoughts, as I did, and you will see what your point of attraction is. Your vibrational state will become clear, and you will see how YOU can change what you bring towards you.

This is another state that has been brand new for me over the past eighteen months, just being with myself. If anyone who knew me only a few years ago is reading this, they will likely notice a drastic shift in my speaking with regards to this topic. As a registered nurse with two science degrees, I was not spiritual in the least. I could not sit still for more than five minutes to do mindfulness activities, let alone half-hour meditations. I always felt like I needed to do and be doing at all times. I started to connect with myself more, and when I did, I began to realize that there is more in this universe than just me in a body. I started to examine my beliefs around how we got here, how we as humans were created, and where we are in relation to this infinite universe. I realized I am infinite. I am connected to this source and supply and I give and receive through this. Many of my beliefs around existence have changed, and thus so have my interactions in this world.

I have connected to spirituality, and I have connected to our source and now receive what I ask for from it. Things don't always need to be explained, and things don't always need to be seen. I am okay with just believing. My faith is great, something I did not have before this past year of growth.

CHAPTER 9

The Universe Speaks

One thing I am getting really good at embracing is my relationship with the source. This is not something I had thought about once just over a year ago. I would have been completely lost if you had asked me what that was. Source, universe, and spirit are all words that were never in my vocabulary before. I truly had no explanation for how I got here, how I interacted within the "universe," or what that even meant.

I remember hearing for the first time, "The universe is transpiring to give you everything you ask for," and thinking, "Are you nuts? What does that even mean?" The more I asked questions, the more I learned, and the more intrigued I became. At first, it started with more tangible explanations like "energy flows through you and into a form to create what you want in life." Then it became things like "asking the universe for guidance." My awareness of this has expanded so much and will likely continue to expand even past when I am writing this. The important thing to note here is my open mind.

The "universe," to me, is our connection to our source. It is what my mind, body, and soul connect into. It is what guides me and what I collaborate with to create my life. I have been given a purpose, and I am simply a vessel through which the universe can work. We are not meant to live in fear, worry, and doubt, and I am here to wake people up to what is really possible in a deep and satisfying sort of way.

I was reading a book by Gabrielle Bernstein called *The Universe Has Your Back*, and I absolutely loved it. She told a story about choosing a sign, something that you see as a message from the universe that you are on the right path. She had chosen an owl and I chose a butterfly. It just came to me, and it was the middle of winter, so the likelihood of seeing one was slim. However, butterflies started showing up in very interesting places. As I was trying to decide if I should transition away from my network marketing business and move over to full-time coaching, my upline gave me a card congratulating me on my coaching success, and on the front was a butterfly. I was worried about disappointing her, so the butterfly was a message from the universe that I was going on the right path, that she would be okay, that no one would be let down.

I started seeing butterflies all over the place: in movies, in emojis that people would send me, in art on the walls, or books on coffee tables. It was obvious in a major way that I was heading towards something truly great and every time I would see one, I would smile, feeling the little nudge to keep going. The day I received two pins from my mentor for achieving levels of excellence in my business, as I left his home, on the patio sliding doors were little butterfly stickers. I knew I was in the right place and that I was meant to be on this journey with him. I saw the butterflies and my heart skipped a beat. A calm rushed over me, knowing that all is going to work out just fine.

There is no need for explanation. There is no need to see everything with our eyes in order for it to exist. This realization was a huge shift for me. I chose to believe this and now everything is different. There are no coincidences. I truly believe the universe is guiding me.

The universe is also speaking to me regularly with numbers. Some refer to them as angel numbers, but to me it's simply a sign. I started seeing 111 as I ventured into my coaching business full time. As I really started to live in what I now truly believe is my purpose, the numbers were everywhere. May 2020 was an incredible training. Everyone was so engaged and inspired and at one point, there were 111 people watching on the live training stream. One person noticed and put 111 in the comments. Then all of a sudden, the chat was flooded with 111. I was so overcome with the signs that I became emotional. THIS IS IT. This is what I am here for. That realization in that moment changed it all.

The morning I reached a goal that I had been working towards for the year, it was a normal Tuesday morning where I teach my clients on Zoom. That morning seemed different, though—people were excited and the energy was stronger. Normally, we have about ninety people online for this early morning session, and about fifteen minutes in, I noticed the participant number was at 111. Of course, I was not the only one to see it, and the chat started filling again with 111. I knew that was the day it was to present itself into my physical world. The universe speaks and I am always listening.

Messages from the universe sometimes come in not-so-nice ways as well. I find that if I am questioning someone or something, the universe will bring it forward for me in order to work through it. We are not meant to hang onto negativity, overwhelm, unorganized thoughts, or indecision. The faster we can sort these things out, the better, and the more purity of mind you will find.

When I look back on times of indecision in my life, I can see how the universe was sending me little nudges or messages to guide me. One of the hardest decisions for me came exactly one year ago. I had decided to become a coach and teach on the topic of mindset. I knew it was what I was supposed to do, that it was my calling. I had been teaching it to my team in network marketing for months and everyone was absolutely loving it. People were changing around me because of my change in beliefs and expanding my knowledge to them. Everyone around me was telling me I needed to be coaching on the topic. I knew it too, but there was this other business and team that I had that I was struggling to let go of. I had built this team over the course of two years, spent so much time and gave so much of myself to it, that I just could not let it go. I had so many friendships, so many team members that relied on me that I really did not want to let anyone down. I kept coming up with ways I could do both at the same time, and grow both businesses. It seemed like there could be a way. But something had shifted inside of me, and I could not connect with the end goal anymore. When I would use my imagination to see myself at a higher level in the network marketing business, I could no longer emotionally connect to it, nor could I hold the picture for very long. I would keep trying, but nothing happened. But when I would picture my coaching business—myself on stage teaching thousands of people, imagining the wins from people I was guiding—my heart sang loudly. There was no doubt about which was my path, so why was I still struggling?

I recognize now that this was my old program that I was not letting go of. The fear of saying goodbye, the worry of what others would think, the indecision around which path is the right one. I remember so clearly the very first sign from the universe about which path I should take. I was in California for our company conference in January. We were enjoying ourselves, but things were different. I recognize now that I had grown so much, I had changed the way I saw things, but others around me had not. Things that I normally would have been fine with were no longer in alignment with this new, higher version of myself (no better than anyone, but my past self). I could feel that I was not as engaged as I used to be, but I felt this overwhelming feeling of not wanting to let anyone down, especially those who meant the most to me. One of my dearest friends and leaders gave out gifts and cards to the team members while we were at our leadership lunch, which was a beautiful gesture. When I opened my card, I was immediately taken aback. The front of the card was a butterfly. I knew this was the universe sending me a message that all was going to be fine and that when I decide to change the course of my life and jump all in with my own business, that she would not be let down, but would be supportive.

You would think that would have been enough to get me moving forward, but it was not. I continued on past the conference, through February. Another sign came when the company conference was announced in Toronto, and it was the exact same weekend as the conference I was hoping to attend for my coaching business. I could not do both and was forced to choose. The choice was an easy one. However, I stayed on longer.

Finally, after a lot of indecision and back and forth, the universe made the decision for me. One of my clients asked me to do a training session for her team. I agreed, and an avalanche of misunderstandings brought forward circumstances that had me finally make the decision to leave. Accusations were made against me, friends and leaders who I was so worried about disappointing turned their back on me, and I knew this was happening for a reason. I was not making the decision I was being guided to, so conflict ensued to create the order that was needed. I was given fourteen days to speak to the allegations against me and while I was drafting up my response, I asked myself for whom I was doing this? I knew my path. I knew my passion and I knew my integrity was intact, so I made the decision to not even respond and to resign my position with the company. So much worry, fear, and indecision, suddenly gone in a moment of pure freedom and pure release.

I am meant to be here, doing this. My other business was a stepping-stone to this, a beautiful gift that served its purpose and I will forever be grateful. I am grateful to the universe for showing me the way, even if it felt harsh at times. I am proud of myself for moving on with grace, for responding and not reacting, and for maintaining my integrity throughout.

CHAPTER 10

Decisions from the End

I learned early on that decision-making alone is a powerful mechanism for success. I have learned to make decisions much quicker and from within much more than I used to. I shifted this by making decisions a certain way, and doing so altered things quickly for me.

If I am using my imagination to go to the end result, where my dreams and desire are fulfilled, then it means that I can tap into that energy, that place where I am confident in my decisions. It would stand to reason then that the decisions I make in that place should be the same decisions I make now in my physical world. If I want the result of a decision to take me to the end, then they should be made from the end.

I remember the first time I tried this. I had just launched my business and I was in LA for an event. I had picked up a few clients and was feeling pretty good. I had not quite paid off my initial investment yet, but my faith that this would be done soon was high. I had a thought: "How cool would it be to go buy my first Louis Vuitton bag on Rodeo Drive?" I really had no idea how much they cost, but I had always wanted one. I had even put the one I wanted on my vision board. The purpose of the vision board is to get clear on the goals, the lifestyle I would be living when all my goals were achieved, and buying a Louis Vuitton purse in LA would certainly be something I would be doing. I knew at that moment I needed to go do it. If I chose not to, then I was sending a message out that I was not sure more clients were coming, that I was not confident in my ability to bring in more money. At the end, when abundance is here, I have several of these bags. So, I took myself in an Uber to Rodeo Drive, spent hours in the store, and bought my very first $4,000 purse. My husband was a little surprised, but he understood that I was working on something big, and this was only the beginning.

You would think I would have stopped there. Nope. I decided to take things one step further and fly home first class. The cost was only $500, but after spending so much on a purse I felt a little tense booking it. I knew I needed to behave NOW like I had what I wanted. I got on that plane, in pod seats as I'd hoped, and there were two very successful coaches who were at the top of their game in first class with me. Nothing happens by accident; it all aligns when we allow it to. It was so empowering. I felt so proud, so calm, prosperous, and so boujee. These emotions were exactly the ones I have now, at the end. (It's not the end anymore, but was at the time.) By experiencing them then, I brought forth all I needed into the physical. If I had been focused on my physical world, my current results, I would not have made either of these decisions and I do not believe I would have the results in life I have in this moment.

I used this method a third time and it started becoming a habit. I had come to a point where I wanted to have someone help me with my marketing, email campaigns, course creation, etc. I connected with Sheena online and her work was exactly what I was looking for. She sent me a proposal with three packages, each a different level of affordability. I was physically in a place where my business was going well. I'd paid off the investment I put in and had hired someone to help me with admin tasks. I had clients coming in and I felt confident in the future of the business and its growth. When I opened the packages and their pricing, I have to admit my first reaction was shock: "This costs how much?" Even the lowest package was way beyond what I expected. I knew right away that even the lowest package was a stretch. I decided I would choose the lowest package and as more business success came in, I would upgrade. Before I told Sheena my choice, I started feeling like this was not the right decision. If I was in a state of faith that my business was going to reach what I was creating in my vision, then why would I be choosing the lower package? I realized I was making this decision based on my physical results, my current state of being. I felt this urge to go into a visualization. I went even further than I had before. I did not just picture a million-dollar business, but multi-millions. I felt the joy, the excitement, the pride in achieving this, and I knew my answer immediately. When I have the business I want, I decide to take the VIP package, and so I did. I believe this decision was a pivotal moment in my growth. It was a moment where I made my first decision from a true place of faith and knowing—knowing that my multi-million-dollar business was on its way to the physical.

As you can imagine now, I think from a different end result. I am avoiding the use of terms that make the end bigger or farther away, because doing so places a limit on what I am capable of. If I think something is too big, or that it will take too long, then it changes how I view it, and how I view it means everything. I want to see things as just around the corner—as easy, as fun and joyous, as something natural—because in this natural state is where the magic happens. When we expect success, it shows up. When we assume we have what we want, it's there. When we believe, we see.

CHAPTER 11

Faith Always Knows

Faith has to be one of my absolute favourite topics. I lived thirty-seven years not really feeling like I had faith in anything, to now living in a place of absolute faith. I would not want it any other way.

A few months into the journey of studying myself, I began to think more deeply about beliefs and what they really meant. As I studied beliefs, I started to ask about faith as well. I started to wonder how faith differs from beliefs, and it led me to read a few books on the topic. What I really started to understand was that my beliefs are simply ideas that I see as truth. I was raised to believe that I should go to university after high school and get a degree, find a job that was needed (so I would always be in a job), and to work my way up the ladder through promotions. So, this is what I did.

Faith, on the other hand, is something completely different. There is power in faith. The more I study faith, the more I fall in love with the idea. My awareness around this topic has changed even in the last six months. I was teaching about facing your fears less than six months ago, helping others to understand fear in order to better manage it, and I had this thought: "I just don't want to talk about fear anymore." By even talking about it, I was giving it power, and I'd had enough. I had a realization that to rid yourself of fear, you need to live in faith. As you move closer to faith, the feeling of fear simply dissipates. So, I decided to place my focus solely on that, as I do with many things I want more of in my life. What we give focus to grows, and what we lose sight of floats away. The problem with most of us is that we let our dreams float away.

The first step towards living in faith was to identify the feeling of faith. Have I experienced this before? Could I draw upon it to be able to use that feeling in another context? I used to believe faith was related to religion, but as I started to study it more, it became very clear that I did have faith, and in a lot of things (even in myself). When I applied to university, I had faith in myself that I would finish it and find a good job. When I accepted a new job, I did so with faith that I would bring a good contribution to the organization. I call an Uber with faith that I will get dropped off at the airport. I put a pot of water on the burner, knowing when I come back it will be boiling. We start families with faith that we will be able to care for our children and give them a good life. When we step outside of our homes and plant our feet on the ground, we do so with faith that gravity will keep us from flying up into the sky. We have faith in this, even though we cannot see it! We have faith that the sun comes up and will go back down at night.

There was so much polarity in the realization that I have been living in faith on an unconscious level. I never even realized it. So why, then, was I having faith in some things, yet no faith in others? There were things that I would not have faith in unless I was able to see it with my own eyes. I would doubt my ability to do anything extraordinary, I would doubt the miraculous healing of disease, and I would consider fast success only for "certain people." I would see other people succeed and think, "I will never do that."

One of my favourite comments on faith from Dr. Robert Russell is when he paraphrases a well-known quote about faith being the actuality of things that we hope for, and the confirmation of things that we cannot see. Something exists in our faith of it. Having faith is having courage—the courage to believe in more than what the masses believe. Faith that you are not just like everyone else, but that you have unique greatness within you. Why fit in when you can stand out and show others how to stand out too?

Much like I think of thought being energy, I also believe faith brings power. The more faith you have, the more powerful you are. It is not enough to simply be in a state of faith; you must be in action with that faith. When in true faith, you act in no other way than that your desires are already here, even if you cannot see them. I entered into this state and the entire world around me changed. Fear now seems small; it feels more like excitement for the growth to come. It no longer becomes a barrier, but rather a sign that I am growing. Faith is what connects the physical and spiritual—a connection I am very grateful for.

Some of the questions I have asked myself over this past year have brought me great strength, as they have me focus on a state of being I want to be in, and not on one I want to avoid. I would ask myself these things: "What would you do if you were in a state of complete and utter faith? How would it feel to believe so deeply in something that taking action towards it is free and limitless, easy and rewarding?" Now I strive every day to be in a state of absolute faith and knowing. How do I know what this feels like? It feels like no one can tell me otherwise, and even my own doubts about it are gone. I am convinced.

CHAPTER 12

My Dominant Feeling

I remember telling my parents when I was growing up that I "can't help how I feel." This is what I truly believed, right up until I was thirty-seven years old. Emotions were something that just happened, and I had to just deal with them. And were they ever powerful around my monthly cycle…watch out! I felt like I had zero control of anything. I was an emotional person and felt sadness on a regular basis. I don't remember much of my childhood or high school years because I was not a very happy person. I didn't have a bad childhood. I was blessed in so many ways, but I always felt less than. I had this desire to fit in, but never felt like I did. I did some things that I'm not proud of because I thought people would like me if I did (as many young people do, I'm sure). One thing I wish I knew back then was that these emotions were modifiable.

Emotion is a choice. Sadness is a choice. Happiness is a choice. I used to say, "I just want to be happy," and then focus on how sad I was.

What is the dominant feeling you are in? That is your success mechanism and point of attraction. It's not about each individual thought; it's the culmination of thoughts that create the result. It's the ideas that are impressed upon the unconscious mind. I used to get so stressed that I developed very real pain in my shoulder. It was like a muscle cramp. I wouldn't be consciously aware of why I was stressed—sometimes I honestly couldn't understand why—but I knew that's what was happening. This dominant feeling that would live in my heart (my unconscious mind) was literally creating pain in my body, and was entirely unconscious on my part. My mind was not filled with worry or doubt, but there was a feeling there.

Ups and downs are normal, but it's when the dominant feeling changes entirely that you want to watch for. I loved this idea. This gave me hope. I don't need to be perfect. I can have some thoughts come in that aren't perfect (because, hey, I'm human!) and everything will still work out how I want it to.

I can now tell immediately when my dominant feeling changes, and it's usually related to something external to myself. I always ask myself, "Am I perceiving this in the most positive way, or could I?" For example, there will always be other people who do or say things that are not very kind, but I know that other people's self-image is what causes them to be harsh towards others. When you are in a loving, calm, and confident space and are truly happy with who you are, you do not make others feel small or less than. You simply accept others no matter what. I choose compassion in these situations and send love their way. This is how I perceive these situations.

CHAPTER 13

Beliefs Into Reality

I have an undergraduate degree in sociology and psychology, so I studied communities, individuals, beliefs, and paradigms; but I never studied them from this perspective before, prior to this recent time in my life. Years of life and work experience definitely helped me in understanding truths a bit better. What I believed while I was in university is very different from what I believe today. My reality is a culmination of my beliefs, so what I believe to be true will be my truth. This past year has been a time where I have been very intentional about my beliefs. Have you ever questioned your beliefs? No? Me neither. What I can tell you for sure is that the me before this past year would have never believed what could be possible *for me* in one year. The key here is *for me*. I could have believed it for someone else, but certainly not for me.

I had a belief that was formed when I was a young girl, and it steered my life in so many ways. As a heavier girl and then adult, I had a belief that because I was overweight, I was inferior. This message was ingrained in me deeply. Every birthday when I would blow out the candle, I would wish to be "skinny." My belief was that being skinny was better, and I aspired to be that. When I dug even deeper, I realized that I not only wanted to be skinny, but I also believed I needed to be skinny to be accepted, to be loved, to achieve success. My physical world was telling me this was true over and over again. I would lose a chunk of weight and receive praise and feel accepted. I met my husband at my lowest weight. And I grew a successful network marketing business after losing 100 lbs. All these things proved my belief to be true.

The sad thing in having this belief is that every single time I gained the weight back, my inferiority came back with it. At one of the heaviest points in my life, when I started really studying myself, I began asking myself the truth behind this belief. As I examined this belief, I started attracting people into my life, confident and successful women who were curvy and loved their bodies. At first it made no sense, because who wouldn't want to be skinny? As I started to change my awareness, it all started to make sense. By continuing to believe this narrative, this story I had rooted inside my heart, I was in a self-made prison, unable to escape unless I met this standard. I made the decision (yes, this is a choice) to change this belief. What would life be like if I did not believe this, if I could be successful in the body I am in right now? I loved the thought of this and decided to nurture this belief instead of my previous one. I replaced the narrative on a conscious level. I told myself the exact opposite of the old belief until it became my truth. Here I am today, plus-size and a millionaire. One belief, changed on purpose, made all the difference. Something that hindered me my entire life was gone, and I was free to express myself fully. This is freedom. Every single thing I have been through has a purpose. The number of women who have reached out to me and told me that they have let their body image impact their success, telling me I threw their paradigm out the window, has shown me that I went through it all for that. I know this. I'm so grateful for the chance to help others see their potential.

There is so much power in taking your beliefs back. We are led to believe that certain things are truth, and likely taught by someone who was taught by someone else who has no idea where it originally came from. Using our reason allows us to actually think and reflect, and to understand why we believe these things. We often have a desire to be like the masses, but if we think like the masses, we will live the same life. I don't know about you, but I want something a bit more extraordinary. So, let's stop accepting so many things as truth just because. When I have a belief that is not serving my interests, I intentionally change it to a new one. I love the idea of nurturing beliefs, like I'm taking care of them. What I'm really doing is suggesting a new belief to my subconscious mind until it just becomes my reality.

I am always asking myself this question (and often will ask others): "Do you want to believe that? Does that belief serve you? What belief would serve you more?"

One of the biggest changes in my beliefs is that my reality is what I choose it to be. If the outside world has done me wrong, if I give the responsibility of managing my feelings to others, then my reality will always be at the mercy of others. My happiness will be determined by others; my success, determined by others; my value, determined by others. The most freeing belief to accept is that YOU are in control of your entire world and you can choose happiness, you can choose love, you can choose success. I feel so much compassion for those who continue to be moulded by their outside world. If only they knew how easy it was to release! One step in the right direction to freedom.

The first step in changing your beliefs is to really understand what you believe. Pay attention to some of the explanations you use for your state of emotion: *My business is not growing because the economy is not the best right now. I am sad because he said hurtful things to me. I am frustrated because my friend never calls me.* All of these things are outside of you. All you need to do is go within yourself. You are your beliefs.

When I started to tell myself that I was good at certain things, those things started to show up in my life. When I started to tell myself that I was good at sales, the sales showed up. When I told myself that I was good at making money, more money came in. When I told myself that I was happy in the body I am in now, I started being happier. *I'm trying to be better, I'm hoping to be good at this,* and *I'm working on showing up more* are all ways of saying that you currently do not believe you are those things. Believe you are NOW and you will be.

CHAPTER 14

I Am So Grateful for…

Gratitude has helped me in so many ways this past year. When I began in network marketing, I was told to write down three things I am grateful for every morning. I did this for a couple of months and didn't notice too much of a difference. It felt like I was doing it just because I was told to, and I never really engaged much in the actual practice of it except for the five minutes it took to write the three things down. I began to really engage in the practice of gratitude about eighteen months ago, and this time I took a very different approach. This time I spent time not only writing down the thing I was grateful for, but actually picturing it and feeling the emotion of having it. This really started to change things for me. This was not about just finding the good in my life, but changing my entire attitude about my life. The biggest difference for me is in actually living in an attitude of gratitude all day long. This is very different than just writing a few things down.

Imagination is a tool for manifesting my dream life, and gratitude is also something I use while in my imagination. Feeling the feeling of the wish being fulfilled is key in the manifestation process and using gratitude during a visualization is very profound. It is a beautiful way of bringing emotion into the visual, but it also helps to feel as though YOU actually have what it is you want. We often "dream" about something and never truly believe we will ever obtain it, but when you visualize it and feel it, your mind thinks it's real. When you think it's real, it happens. When I am in my imagination with all my goals achieved, I take a look around in that moment and see all the amazing things to be grateful for: my success, my relationships, my support, my environment, my experiences, my time and financial freedom, etc. I am almost always grateful for myself for never giving up.

Fourth-dimensional gratitude is a practice I do every morning. I write down five things I am grateful I have in my physical world (the visible) and five things I am grateful for that are on their way.

Gratitude is also helpful in being able to find the good in every situation. When negative things show up in my life, I am able to reflect back and ask myself, "What am I grateful for in this?" Usually, I find clarity or order in tough situations, and in those situations, I find the growth I needed to reach that next level. Growth is required, and once I realize this, then I recognize how grateful I am for the challenge, for the perceived setback, and for the lesson that is showing up for me.

Vishen Lakhiani talks about living in a blissful state now in order to manifest your dream life. You can't be unhappy with what you have and manifest what you want. The law of vibration proves this. I love this idea and I make sure I am in this peak state of joy and bliss.

CHAPTER 15

Giving All Around

Generosity has been a huge component of why I believe I was able to receive so much abundance this year. I have always been someone who is caring and always wanted to help others, so nursing was the obvious career path when I couldn't figure out what else I wanted to do. As I started to study myself, things started clicking for me, and other people could see it too. They saw the alignment, the flow opening, and the change in me. I was showing up more confidently, expressing my expertise in the material I was studying, and achieving success. This is when people started reaching out to me for help—potential clients, current clients, other coaches, the general public. The reaction became overwhelming at times, but the more people I helped, the more questions I answered, the more other people started seeing success. And with their success came more for me.

A few months back, I introduced a strategy into my business that worked very well. We found it online and gave it a try. We adopted our own way of doing it and because I was in a state of flow and alignment, and had the right thinking behind it, it worked like a charm. Other coaches started asking me for tips and tricks and to share my strategy. In an industry of coaching, especially where we all work within the same context, some would have kept their strategies to themselves. I decided to be open and honest and help anyone who wanted to know more. I taught people individually, then as a group, and others started to really succeed at it!

This raised my vibration and had me feeling empowered and satisfied that I was able to make an impact on people. I felt blessed to be able to do this for others. I understand that I was simply the vehicle for them to receive what they needed, but being that vehicle is truly an honour. I built a massively successful business for myself, have been part of facilitating others to do the same, and now even my mentor uses my strategy after I brought it to his company. This is the kind of impact I wanted to make, and here I am, receiving abundantly.

This proves that I have truly been in the collaborative and creative plane, which is never competing with us. Competition can bring about feelings of lack or unworthiness. I choose to compete only with my past best. While the urge to compete is there, I replace this with a giving heart.

Another thing I am very generous with is my time. I found that by doing above and beyond what was expected of me allowed me to receive more. As I express my energy, the more impact I am able to make. The further my energy reaches, the more I can help others. It is my desire to help others reach what I have that drives me. My biggest weakness right now is that I want to give everyone my time, but cannot. I choose to leverage it and speak to more people at one time.

CHAPTER 16

Money

The topic of money is something I could likely speak for days on. The way in which I view the concept of money has shifted tremendously. I no longer look at others and want the same with this longing that I will never have it. I never feel like money is lacking—if anything, I now believe there is more than enough to go around. The important thing to note here is that this feeling changed before the money came, not the other way around.

Money was something I never felt like I had much of. Anytime we had money, it would be spent and then would take a long time to build back up again. It always felt like we just never had enough. I enjoyed spending money, but felt like I could never spend large amounts on things. I remember going shopping and trying on a bunch of clothes, and once I got the total at the checkout, I would take two items out to make the price lower. I did this every time. It was as if spending under $200 was acceptable, but nothing more. I would see people with designer bags who weren't making as much money as me and think, "How can they afford that?" It never made sense to me. I did not grow up struggling for things. My parents were able to provide well for me, especially as I got into my teenage years, but I realize that I did believe money was hard to make. I had worked some jobs for not a lot of money that I disliked very much. I began to be driven by more than dollars; I was driven by the internal satisfaction that came with it. I pursued a nursing career that would earn good money—or so I thought. I remember working sixteen-hour overnight shifts, exhausted when I got home. I'd see the paycheck and think, *this is it?*

I believed that in order to make more money, I needed a higher-level degree, a promotion, to work overtime, or to start a second business. So, I did all of the above. I never saw myself making more than $140K per year. I would look at the pay scale as a nurse and think to myself, *I guess if I want to make more money, I need to be the CEO*, and that was a job I certainly did not want. They had so much pressure on them, were overworked, and never smiled! I felt stuck. I could not see any way of making money other than the way I was doing it in that moment. My vision was limited and so were my options. What I failed to recognize is that my job was only the mechanism for the money to flow to me, and that by seeing the thousands of other ways to do it, I would open a whole new world. This started my journey to entrepreneurship.

Things had an okay start. I saw some initial successes and then things remained stagnant. Even as my own business grew, I never seemed to make more money than my biggest month of $10k. What I know now is that I was set to make no more than that ever, because I did not allow myself to visualize it. My belief started to shift pretty quickly once I started to learn about the power of the mind and thoughts on money. I changed how I saw money. Instead of focusing on the lack of it and barely watching it grow, I shifted my focus to thinking of more of it. I will never forget my first experience really playing around with this idea, when I manifested money to the extra dollar.

After one month into studying the power of the mind, I decided to make a goal of bringing in $20k per month. I had never made more than about $8k per month, and that was with a full-time job and a side business. I was down to just the side business, so this goal seemed impossible. I was told not to try to figure out "how" it would happen, but just to ask for what I wanted. I started writing this out: "I'm so happy and grateful now that I am making over $20k per month easily and continuously." I started using my imagination to picture myself seeing the money in the bank account. As I did this, I realized that the bank account would likely have some money in it, so after the $20k goes in, it will have more. I chose the amount of $21,795. I wrote this number out over and over. I thought about what I would spend it on and pictured that amount in the bank, and focused on how it would feel to have it. About a month later, as I continued thinking the money was on its way, my husband called and told me he had a few stock options that we could exercise if we wanted. I said sure, and never thought much more of it. He called me a week later while I was away at an event in Florida and told me to check the bank as the money should have been deposited. I logged into my online banking and my heart started racing immediately. There was $21,795.85 in my bank account. It worked! Holy shit, this works! I believed before, but now I *really* believed. I called my coach Danielle and she told me to add a zero. So I did...and here I am with income well past that amount each month!

The ironic part of this story is that I am now a CEO (the role I had previously dreaded) of my own company, working from home, making more money in some weeks than I made in six months. And I am not stressed, not overwhelmed, and I feel so blessed for the work I do. I do some things now that would not have made sense to me before. When I have a desire to bring more money in, maybe a business goal or for a purchase, I express energy through the exchange of money. I usually make a purchase—a large one. This makes it known that I expect more money to be coming. This works every single time. I spend money on things to bring more money towards me. I have fun with this. I remember thinking that I had a big goal in the month of September and hadn't spent much money lately. I felt the urge to do something, so I ordered a Gucci purse. It arrived during my conversion event, and I ended up enrolling more clients in that month than in any previous month. Coincidence? Nope.

One of the things I am most proud of is my new home. I had developed a really clear idea of the type of home I wanted to move into, and I knew exactly where I wanted to live. The house we were in was too small and my energy had grown out of it. We had downsized when my business was not going well, so it was something that I was disappointed in myself for. It took eight months to manifest my dream home. When we found the home, it first felt far out of reach. It had more than we wanted. It is a bungalow and has a theatre, a gym, six-car garage, and a glassed-in office. It had all the bells and whistles and was for sale for much more money than we had. I knew that what I needed to do was show the universe I was open to receiving and place an offer on the home. I did not have the down payment—not even close. But, as I now know, if I ask, I will receive. Could offering on the home help me bring in more money and make my business grow at the same time? Yes, I believe this is true. So, we did it. We made an offer on the home and had forty-five days to manifest a large sum of money (let's just say it was in the hundreds of thousands of dollars). There were very brief moments of "what are we thinking," but for the most part, I kept my focus strictly on us living in the home. I spent most of my days there, in the fourth dimension. I was physically in the old house, but psychologically I was living in the new one. There was no doubt that this was our home and that we would be moving in soon. We stayed the course, packed up, made arrangements with movers, and planned for it all. This was a beautiful experience, showing myself what I was truly capable of. We ended up making more money than we needed, and moved into our dream home at the end of October 2020.

Moving into the new home became a new paradigm, a new level of wealth, to grow myself more into the person I want to become. When we wait until things feel secure, until we have it all figured out, or until it feels "safe," it comes from a place of lack and a place of fear. I choose faith over fear every single day. I know my current world is my past thinking, and what I am thinking right now (which is my future) is really, really big.

The funny thing about my year and the manifestation of money is how fun and lively the whole thing was. I remember being asked to speak at an online event in the middle of July with Bob Proctor and he interviewed me on my success. He was shocked to hear that I had brought one million dollars of income into my household through my business in just seven months. I really started to realize that most people don't do this…although I expected to for some reason? Why don't we expect or think this will happen to us? He asked me what is next, and my first thought was, *Well, I just did one million dollars in seven months, so I think I can finish the year off at two million.* As I started to say it to him, I realized right away that this involved no growth. There was no stretch. So I immediately said three million dollars by the end of the year. I had no clue how I was going to do this, but I believed I could, and that I wanted to. He pushed me to think bigger, and this is why it happened. I know for a fact that we limit ourselves in so many ways.

What I know for certain is that I changed my relationship with money, and more money came. Makes total sense.

CHAPTER 17

Personal Power

In the introduction of this book, I talked about how my powers showed up when I started to really believe in myself. A year ago, I would have never even used the term "power," and if I did, I would have meant it in a negative way, as in people wanting more "power" over others. That is a pretty good indication of where my thinking was. I saw the concept of power as something someone has over another person. Wow…I see things so differently now. Power is something we have within, something we can choose to utilize or not.

Over the course of the past year, my personal power has grown so much that I have no doubt about what I am capable of. The word "power" alone evokes a positive emotion in me now, because I know I am full of power; I am powerful. That was one of the first affirmations I created for myself not too many months ago. What could be better than believing you are powerful? I can't think of anything, if I'm being totally honest. To be powerful means to let go, to release force, and use the strength that is within.

I first acknowledged my power when I realized that I have been building (and will continue to build) my physical reality around me. I also have the power to choose how I perceive my physical surroundings. I began asking myself really good questions, like, "What would I love? How would I like this to go?"

I practiced this power for the first time when I used my mind to win a contest, intentionally. I had been studying the mind for only a short time and thought I would have some fun with it. I entered into a contest with my company to win a chance to interview a top leader. There was a qualification amount of sales needed, and those who qualified would be entered into a draw. I figured I would give it a go. I took pen to paper and wrote down what I would love to happen. I wrote about the moment I found out that I won the contest, how fun the interview was, and how grateful I was for winning it. This formed a picture in my mind right away: I could see myself winning, and the feeling of joy rushed over me. That's what I did before the contest even began. Well, a week later, I qualified for the contest—and of course, my name was pulled from the draw!

I kept doing this, testing out my power. I began getting increasingly more specific with what I wanted to happen.

What would I love to see in my future? I thought to myself, *it would be really nice to be a best-selling author*. I never thought about writing a book before, but now the thought of it sounded nice. It was one of about fifty things I would love to see in my future. Wouldn't you know it, the very next day I was asked to co-author a chapter in a book on self-love. Eight months later it hit the top seller list. The more I started asking for things, the more they started to happen. I began to think more about the business of my dreams, and I decided I wanted to have one person join my team per day. Can you guess what happened? After thinking about it for a couple of weeks and believing it was possible, I began recruiting at a rate of one person per day. I later used this exact same method to bring in one high-ticket client per day. It really does not matter if what you want is considered too big or too small—it all manifests in the exact same way.

My belief in the power of the mind grew even stronger as my clients started to see their own success. One of my very first clients did something in a period of three months that would take others years to do. She completed quantum leaps in her results in her business and in her finances, and it all happened so quickly that before she knew it, she needed a new goal. Another client manifested the cost of the program to work with me the day after she enrolled, to the dollar amount. This has happened about six times now, and it is not a coincidence. Seeing people step into their power like this is the new norm in my world, and these events have all begun to happen with regularity since I stepped into my personal power. Those who believe, those who do as suggested, and those who remain in a state of fun get what they ask for. And those who do this always have an impact on others. Wins in my community come regularly. They often seem magical, but I know they are actually happening because that person believed in their power, just as I believe in my own.

I continue to use this power inside me. Just last week I did a manifestation that was quite simple. I was getting used to having 1200 people register for my training sessions. It was comfortable, and I knew I could continue to fill a training of this size. But as I went into this month's training, I again thought to myself, *what would I love?* I thought to myself that I would love 3500 people registered this time. I wrote that number down, expressed it to a couple of people on my team, and the process had begun. Everything I needed for that to transpire in the physical world began to happen. The universe aligned, and we ended up reaching 3500 registrants the day of the training. The most important thing I've learned from each of these situations is to think bigger and ask for more. Why stop at the 3500 mark?

The key to our personal power is that we must see it and acknowledge it. I can't help you if you are blind to it—just like Neo in *The Matrix*. He believed, and he did. I have gotten very good at asking and receiving. The timing is not relevant for me anymore because I know it is happening. Sometimes it comes quick and other times it takes more time, but it always comes. In the grand scheme of things, does time really matter? When we lose patience, when we lose hope and become impatient, we have moved into resistance and are no longer receiving. If you knew without the shadow of a doubt that everything you wanted was on its way, you would patiently sit and wait while enjoying the life you have at this moment. It's that simple.

Conclusion

What does becoming "the one" mean to me?

Becoming "the one" means so many things. It's being the one and only me. When I started to see uniqueness as my power is when I began to truly love myself for me, instead of trying to be like everyone else and trying to fit in. A fellow powerful woman and friend, Kathrin, recently said to me, "It's never about fitting in; it's always about what fits us." I could not agree more. We all need to be reminded of this over and over again.

Becoming "the one" means taking responsibility. I am the only one who can change my circumstances. Instead of looking for things outside myself, I go inside and work on growth, on my thinking, and get back to asking for what I would love. I am the one who now accepts her power and grows it along my journey.

Being "the one" also means believing that I have a purpose, a reason for being here on earth, in this body, to awaken and enlighten others to different beliefs, different views on reality, different ways of living—ones without struggle.

Someone asked me this question last week and I think it's such a perfect one: If you could suggest one thing to do every single day to achieve success, what would that be? My answer was simple. Trust. Trust in you, and trust in the universe.

Acknowledgements

This book would not have been done, and certain not as quickly as it was, without Peggy McColl. An intuitive hit to send her a text message only a few months ago, led to one of the most inspired times of my life, putting pen to paper to tell my story.

There would be no book, no story to tell without the loving support of my husband. You were open to my crazy ideas, supported our household while I went "inside," and continue to be by my side as we build our dream life together and our legacy for our daughters.

The woman I am today, the one who believes in herself, the one who believes in her purpose, is a combination of two incredible people, my parents. Their quest for more became mine, and I am forever grateful for the example I have been so honoured to expand upon.

Every step of my journey was paved with those who trusted in me, those who followed my lead, and those who had faith in me. My clients and my Diamond Academy team are in every page of this book.

Lastly, my awakening was only possible because of one man who committed his life to the potential hidden within all of us, Mr. Bob Proctor. You paved the way for me to follow in your footsteps, and I am eternally grateful.

About the Author

Kathleen Cameron is a Manifestation Queen, Success Coach, 7 figure entrepreneur, and record breaking author. In just 18 months, she has built a 6 million dollar business and continues to share her knowledge and expertise with all of whom she connects with.

With her determination, unwavering faith, and powers of manifestation, she has helped over 100,000 people attract more love, money, and success into their lives. Her innovative approaches to Manifestation and utilizing the Laws of Attraction have led to the creation of one of the top global success networks.

Through Diamond Academy Coaching, thousands of students have been able to experience quantum growth. The force behind her magnetic field has catapulted many students into a life beyond their wildest dreams and she is just getting started.

Kathleen is a mother of two wonderful daughters, graduated with two undergraduate degrees and a Master's degree, has held a high level executive position in healthcare, and transferred her knowledge to so many others in a way that brings everyone's vibrations up alongside hers.

Resources

Millionaire Academy

Through this 12-week Millionaire Academy Program, you will learn to truly embody what it is to think, feel, and behave like a millionaire. You will learn how to make decisions from a place of already having everything you could ever want. You will learn to dream bigger than you have ever allowed yourself before (and then some!). And you will learn exactly what it takes to be truly abundant. Kathleen takes learners on a journey to quantum leaping with the duality between spirituality and peak performance.

Diamond Academy Coaching Program

This 6-month coaching program (and 3-month launch support) is for those wanting to become coaches or for existing coaches wishing to level up their business. Every independent Diamond Academy Coach has the opportunity to license and use the Millionaire Academy Program in their coaching packages and offerings. Kathleen has created a road map for coaches to create the identity of a highly successful coach, understand leadership, coaching modalities and change mechanics while receiving the business support for growing and leveraging success in business.

Thinking Into Results Program

The Thinking Into Results Program guides you through a powerful 12-lesson process for creating your new, desired results. Each lesson builds upon the previous lesson. It is important to periodically review the program in its entirety for constant reinforcement of the ideas. It is through the repetition of the lessons that you will experience permanent changes. This transformative program paired with Kathleen's coaching cannot be duplicated and acts as a foundation to building your millionaire mind.

Resources

Guided Visualizations

https://www.diamondacademy.ca/guided-visualizations

You tube

★ YouTube: https://www.youtube.com/channel/UCjsVtfQBbHwfybcLIcnxEMA

Social Media

★ Facebook: https://www.facebook.com/kathleen.cameron.73
★ Instagram: @kathleencameron_formygirls
★ Pinterest: https://www.pinterest.ca/kathleencameron_successcoach/_created/
★ LinkedIn: https://www.linkedin.com/in/kathleen-cameron-4b041833/
★ TikTok: @kathleencameronmanifests

HEARTS to be HEARD

Giving a Voice to Creativity!

With every donation, a voice will be given to the creativity that lies within the hearts of our children living with diverse challenges.

By making this difference, children that may not have been given the opportunity to have their Heart Heard will have the freedom to create beautiful works of art and musical creations.

Donate by visiting

HeartstobeHeard.com

We thank you.

Printed in Great Britain
by Amazon

62907199R00061